# Hey Presto!
## Music theory for cellists
### Book 1

1

Georgia Vale

# Hey Presto!

## Music theory for cellists

# Book 1

Published by Hey Presto Strings, Bromsgrove, Worcs
www.heyprestostrings.com

Printed and bound in England, by Pace Print & Design, Worcester
Design of the characters Presto, Bravo and Poco, by Nathalie Walters

# Contents

# The stave and the treble clef sign

Hello, I'm Presto! This is a stave.

This is a **bass clef**. It goes at the start of every line. Bravo will tell you more!

1. How many lines are in a stave?..............

2. Trace over these bass clefs.

Some people call it an **F clef**, as the dots go around the line where F goes.

← F

3. Trace the first two bass clefs, then draw some more of your own.

I'm Poco. I can't draw...

# Bars & bar lines

Music is divided into **bars** using **bar lines**.

A **double bar** is always put at the end of a piece of music.

bar     bar     bar

bar lines

double bar

1. What is the other name for a bass clef? *An F clef*

2. What are these called?

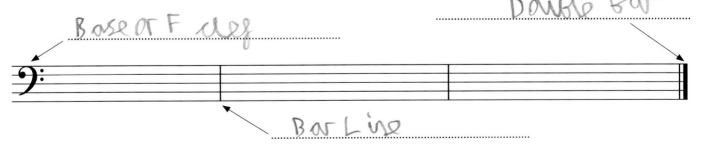

*Base or F clef*

*Double bar*

*Bar Line*

# Space notes

Some notes go on the spaces between the lines. These are called **space notes**.

1. Trace this note on the 1st space, then draw 3 more the same.

2. Trace this note on the 2nd space, then draw 3 more the same.

3. Trace this note on the 3rd space, then draw 3 more the same.

4. Trace this note on the 4th space, then draw 3 more the same.

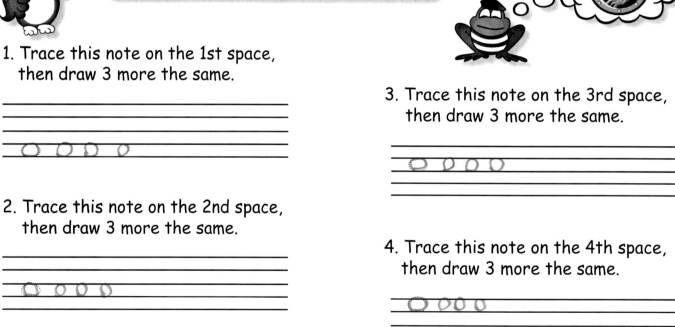

# Line notes

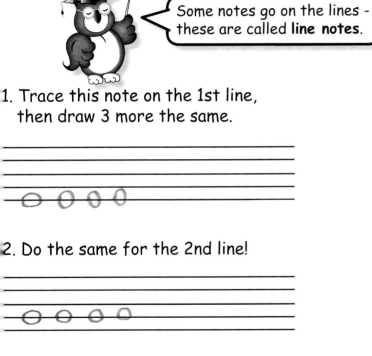

Some notes go on the lines - these are called **line notes**.

1. Trace this note on the 1st line, then draw 3 more the same.

2. Do the same for the 2nd line!

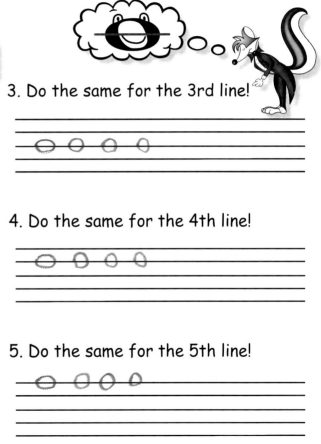

3. Do the same for the 3rd line!

4. Do the same for the 4th line!

5. Do the same for the 5th line!

5

# Time values

**crotchet**

**1 beat**

**minim**

**2 beats**

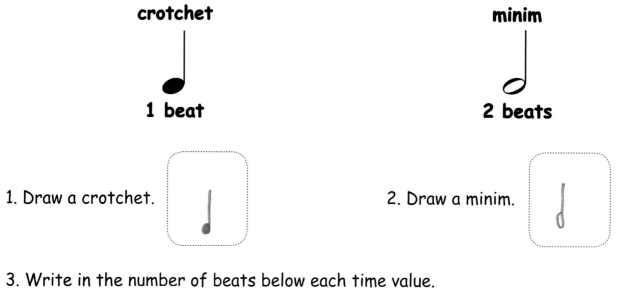

1. Draw a crotchet.

2. Draw a minim.

3. Write in the number of beats below each time value.

**2**   1   1   2   1   2

# More time values

**dotted minim**

3 beats

**semibreve**

4 beats

1. Draw a dotted minim.

2. Draw a semibreve.

3. Write in the number of beats below each time value.

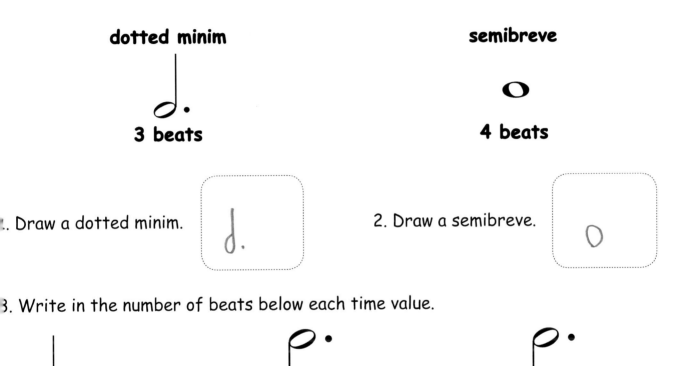

**3**   4   3   4   3

# Even more time values!

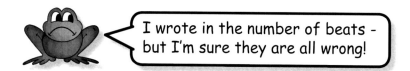

I wrote in the number of beats - but I'm sure they are all wrong!

One, two, three, four, is it less or is it more?

Mark Poco's work - use a tick if it's right or a cross if it's wrong.

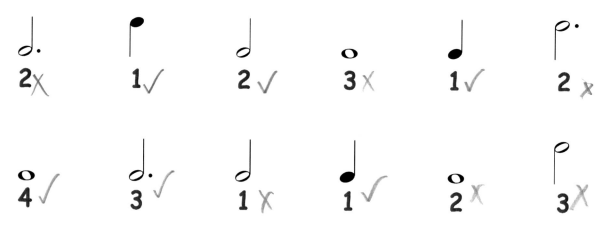

# Bowing directions

This means down bow: ⊓
Pull the bow this way: ☞

This means up bow: V
Push the bow this way: ☞

The bow is quite a special tool,
⊓ V ⊓ V - that's the rule.
⊓ ⊓ V V won't work well -
so do it right and you'll excel!

Write the correct bowing sign above each note marked with a ✲.

# Leger lines

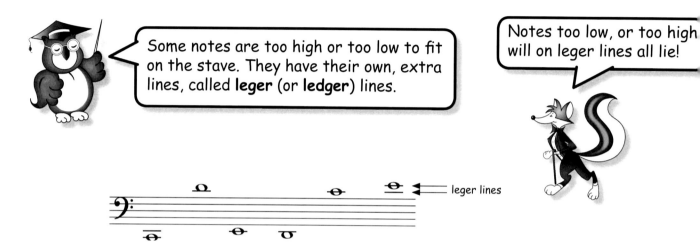

Some notes are too high or too low to fit on the stave. They have their own, extra lines, called **leger** (or **ledger**) lines.

Notes too low, or too high will on leger lines all lie!

leger lines

Put a ring around the notes with leger lines.

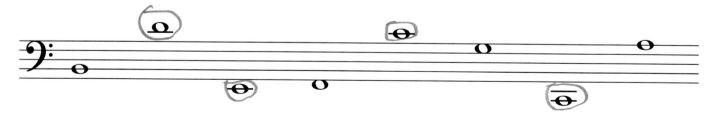

# Drawing leger lines

Look at these leger lines - some are right, some are wrong.

Are they right or are they wrong?
Are they sloping or too long?
Much too low or much too high -
where do you think the line should lie?

Mark Poco's leger lines - a tick if right, a cross if wrong.

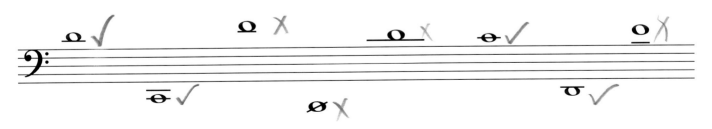

# More line and space notes

**What about notes on leger lines...?**

**Easy! If a note has a line through its face, it's a line note. If not, it's a space note!**

## 1. Put a ring around the space notes.

## 2. Put a ring around the line notes.

# The four cello strings

For music notes we use the letters A to G.
The four cello strings use the notes **C**, **G**, **D** and **A**.

Um... this helps me to remember.

Calm  Goats  Don't  Attack!

Write the name of each string underneath its note.

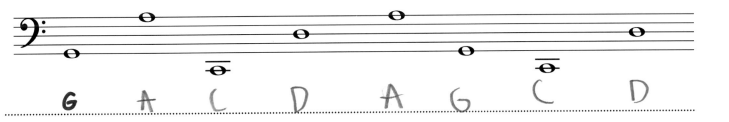

G    A    C    D    A    G    C    D

13

# Stems

Above the middle, letter "p," below the middle, letter "d"!

Heh heh, remember "pod"!

stem

p     o     d

middle

above the middle: stem down, like "p."

below the middle: stem up, like "d."

on the middle: "p" or "d."

middle

Some of Bravo's stems are wrong. Put a ring around the wrong ones.

# Drawing stems

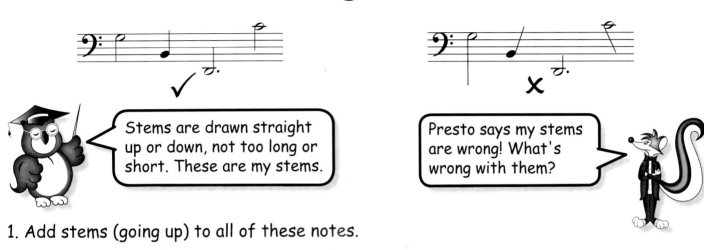

Stems are drawn straight up or down, not too long or short. These are my stems.

Presto says my stems are wrong! What's wrong with them?

1. Add stems (going up) to all of these notes.

2. Add stems (going down) to all of these notes.

# Rests

| crotchet rest | minim rest | dotted minim rest | semibreve rest |
|:---:|:---:|:---:|:---:|
| 1 beat | 2 beats | 3 beats | 4 beats<br>or a *whole bar* |

1. How many beats in each rest?

..........................................................................................................................................................

2. Which rest is used for a whole bar? .........................................................................................................

3. Which rest is worth 2 beats? ...................................................................................................................

# Drawing rests

1. Draw three minim rests.

Help! Which is which?

2. Draw three semibreve rests.

**M**inim rests are like **m**otorboats, floating *on top* of the line.
**S**emibreve rests are like **s**ubmarines, sinking *under* the line!

They both go into the same space! Look:

3. Trace over Presto's crotchet rests, then draw four more.

sloping letter 'z's     sloping letter 'c's                    1     2     3     4

# More of the four cello strings

I wrote the names of these strings under the notes, but I bet they're all wrong. Presto wants you to put a ring around the wrong ones...

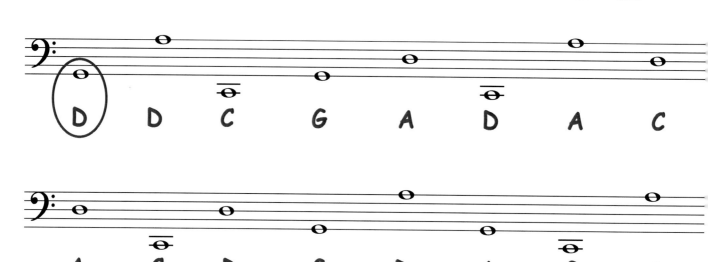

# More time values and rests

1. Draw the rest to match this note. 𝅗𝅥

2. Draw a note which lasts for 4 beats.

3. Draw the note ( ♩ 𝅗𝅥 𝅗𝅥. 𝅝 ) to match this rest. 𝄾

Oh no! I can't remember!

4. How many beats are there in a dotted minim? ..............................................................

5. How many beats are there in this rest? ..............................................................

6. What is this called? ♩ ..............................................................

7. Draw the rest which is used for a whole bar.

8. How many of these ♩ will fit into one of these 𝅗𝅥 ? ..............................................................

# Notes by step

Notes use the alphabet -
A to G - don't forget!

C D E F G A B C D E F G A B C

STOP
LOOK

1. Which note is above A?

2. Which note is above G?

3. Which note is above C?

4. Which note is above F?

5. Which note is above B?

6. Which note is below E?

7. Which note is below D?

8. Which note is below A?

9. Which note is below C?

10. Which note is below F?

# More notes by step

1. These notes go up one step at a time. Write in their names.

C

2. These notes go down one step at a time. Write in their names.

D

# Time signatures - the top number

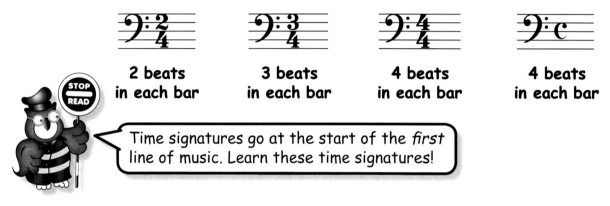

**2 beats in each bar**  **3 beats in each bar**  **4 beats in each bar**  **4 beats in each bar**

c = 4/4

Time signatures go at the start of the *first* line of music. Learn these time signatures!

1. How many beats in each bar?

2. Draw a time signature of 3 beats.

3. Draw a time signature of 4 beats.

# Time signatures - the bottom number

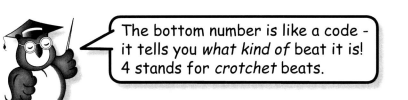

The bottom number is like a code - it tells you *what kind of* beat it is! 4 stands for *crotchet* beats.

3 *crotchet* beats per bar

2 *crotchet* beats per bar

1. What does $\frac{2}{4}$ mean? ................................................................................................................................

2. What does $\frac{4}{4}$ mean? ................................................................................................................................

3. What does C mean? ................................................................................................................................

4. Choose the correct words, and shade them in any colour you like!

, $\frac{3}{4}$ and $\frac{4}{4}$ are all

| time |
| key |
| beat |

signatures. The

| middle |
| bottom |
| top |

number tells you how many

| notes |
| crotchets |
| beats |

are in each bar.

The

| middle |
| bottom |
| top |

number tells you what kind of beat it is. So $\frac{2}{4}$ means 2 crotchet beats per bar, and $\frac{3}{4}$ means

3

| minim |
| semibreve |
| crotchet |

beats per bar. C is just another way to say $\frac{2}{4}$ $\frac{3}{4}$ $\frac{4}{4}$ . Time signatures only go on the

| first |
| second |
| third |

line.

# Bravo's matching pairs

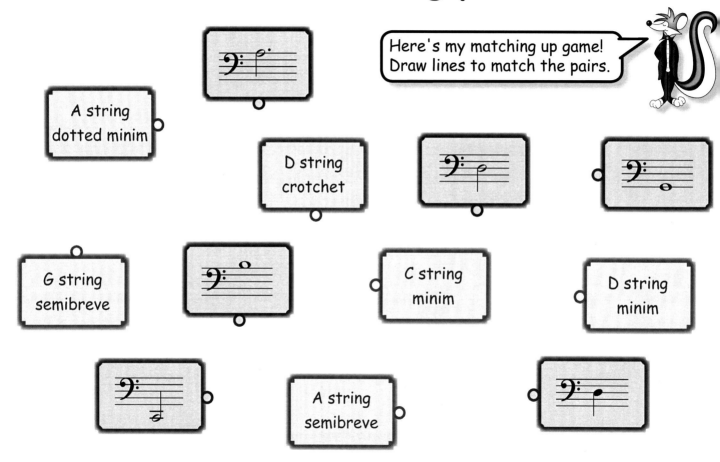

# More time signatures

Poco has written some music - but does each bar add up to the right number of beats? Will you mark his work for him?

1. ................. crotchet beats per bar

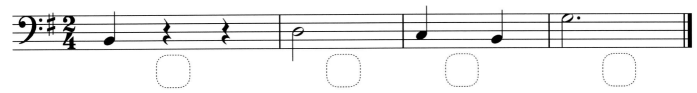

2. ................. crotchet beats per bar

3. ................. crotchet beats per bar

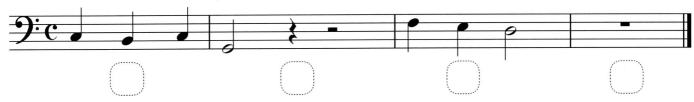

# Accidentals

1. Draw a sharp here.

2. Draw a flat here.

3. Draw a natural here.

4. Which accidental lowers a note? ......................................................................................

5. Which accidental cancels out another one? ......................................................................................

6. Which accidental raises a note? ......................................................................................

# Drawing accidentals

Accidentals are drawn just *before* the note.
They go around the same space or line as the note.

A flat    F natural    G sharp

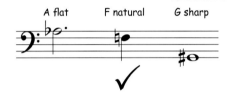 ✓

 ✗

## 1. Trace these notes and accidentals.

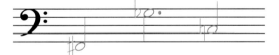

## 2. Copy each note and accidental.

## 3. Some of Bravo's accidentals are wrong. Put a ring around the wrong ones!

# More about accidentals

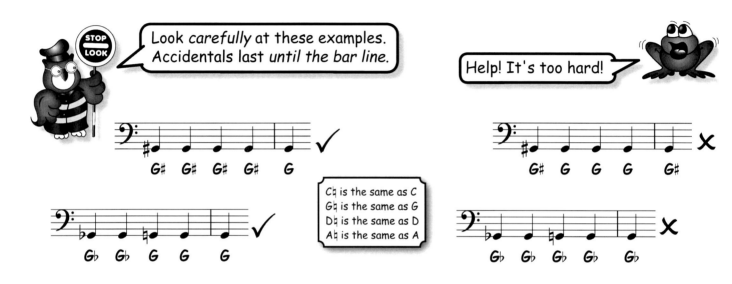

**Look *carefully* at these examples. Accidentals last *until the bar line*.**

**Help! It's too hard!**

C♮ is the same as C
G♮ is the same as G
D♮ is the same as D
A♮ is the same as A

Name each note marked with a ☆ above it.

F#

# Musical maths!

Poco has added up some notes. Will you mark them for him?

Pages 5, 6 and 15 will help!

▬ is the same as ▬

▬ is the same as ▬

# More leger lines

Bravo has drawn notes with leger lines, but he's been careless! Will you put a ring around the wrong ones?

Now copy these notes with leger lines.

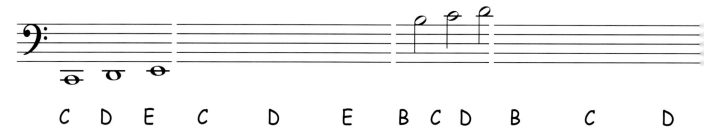

C    D    E        C        D        E    B  C  D    B        C        D

# Even more notes by step!

Shh! Don't tell Presto - I started to draw notes going up and down one step at a time, but I got bored! Will you finish them for me?

Pages 19 and 20 will help!

C  D  E                    D

G  F  E  D  C  B  A  G  F

G        C        C  B  A  G

# Dynamics

Dynamics tell you how loud or quiet to play. They are Italian words!

| | | |
|---|---|---|
| *f* forte | = loud | |
| *ff* fortissimo | = very loud | |
| *mf* mezzo forte | = moderately (quite) loud | |

| | | |
|---|---|---|
| *p* piano | = soft (quiet) | |
| *pp* pianissimo | = very soft | |
| *mp* mezzo piano | = moderately soft | |

1. Put these dynamics in order, starting with the loudest.

    *mp*    *f*    *pp*    *ff*    *mf*    *p*

    ............  ............  ............  ............  ............  ............

2. Which sign means very loud?

3. What does *pp* stand for?

4. Which sign means soft?

5. Write the Italian for moderately loud.

................................................................    ................................................................

# Poco's birthday present

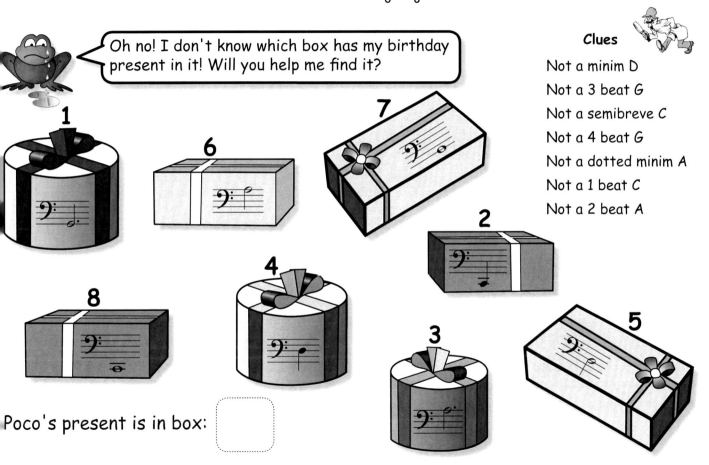

Oh no! I don't know which box has my birthday present in it! Will you help me find it?

**Clues**

Not a minim D

Not a 3 beat G

Not a semibreve C

Not a 4 beat G

Not a dotted minim A

Not a 1 beat C

Not a 2 beat A

Poco's present is in box:

# Jumbled notes

C D E F G A B C D E F G A B C

I spent ages tidying these notes, and now Bravo has dropped them! Will you label them 1 to 10, starting with the lowest note?

# The missing bar lines

Umm... I got hungry and ate some bar-lines!
Please draw them back in for me?

Pages 5, 6 and
15 will help!

1. ............... crotchet beats in each bar

2. ............... crotchet beats in each bar

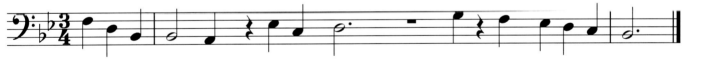

3. ............... crotchet beats in each bar

# Even more accidentals

Sharps ♯ raise notes: D♯ sounds higher than D.
Flats ♭ lower notes: D♭ sounds lower than D.
Naturals ♮ cancel ♯s and ♭s: D♮ is the same as D!

Pages 25, 26 and 27 will help!

1. Put a ring around the higher note of each pair.

2. Put a ring around the lower note of each pair.

3. Name each note marked with a ✮ above it.

# Bravo's secret code

Can you crack my code?

### Code-breaking clues

| | | | |
|---|---|---|---|
| moderately soft | k | time signature | t |
| bass clef | e | sharp | i |
| minim rest | l | soft (quiet) | y |
| very soft | s | stave | h |
| crotchet rest | o | very loud | f |
| loud | n | semibreve | w |
| moderately loud | b | crotchet | d |
| dotted minim | u | up bow | p |
| down bow | v | flat | g |
| natural | r | minim | a |

# Word search

| S | H | A | R | P | D | O | S | T | E | M | L | O | T |
|---|---|---|---|---|---|---|---|---|---|---|---|---|---|
| E | S | O | T | S | E | R | G | N | I | W | O | B | N |
| M | F | A | T | T | T | N | H | N | E | O | R | A | Y |
| I | E | T | A | H | E | A | I | N | I | T | T | S | M |
| B | U | L | C | H | E | M | V | L | A | U | S | S | L |
| R | F | E | L | C | E | L | B | E | R | T | P | I | A |
| E | D | C | T | E | E | R | N | A | T | A | O | E | T |
| V | O | I | E | L | G | O | L | E | C | E | B | N | N |
| E | W | S | H | A | T | E | N | E | S | R | R | O | E |
| L | N | U | C | E | N | U | R | N | T | E | O | T | D |
| I | B | M | T | W | T | V | I | L | R | O | S | I | I |
| N | O | D | O | T | T | E | D | M | I | N | I | M | C |
| E | W | L | R | A | B | I | N | M | N | N | N | E | C |
| U | S | I | C | W | O | B | P | U | G | C | E | S | A |

When you find these words, shade in their letters.

| | | |
|---|---|---|
| semibreve | flat | space |
| up bow | line | semitone |
| accidental | note | rosin |
| music | tune | crotchet |
| sharp | rest | bowing |
| dotted minim | stem | minim |
| leger line | bar | natural |
| bar line | stave | beat |
| down bow | string | |

and **treble clef** - a clef you'll use later!

Write the left-over letters here, to get Presto's secret message (start top left):

_____ , _____ - _____ ,

_____ !

# Spot the difference

There are 15 differences between these pieces of music.
How many can you spot? Put a ring around each one!

# Quiz 1 - test yourself!

1. What is this called? ♩ ................................................................................................

2. How many beats are there in this rest? 𝄽 .............................................................

3. Draw a minim.

4. What note is this (e.g. C, G etc?) 𝄢 ......................................................

5. Which rest is worth 2 beats? ............................................................................

6. How many crotchets fit into a semibreve? ......................................................

7. What does this sign mean? ∨ ............................................................................

8. What does this sign mean? ⊓ ............................................................................

9. Add a stem to this note. 𝄢 ................................................................

10. Name the four cello strings. ............................................................................

# Quiz 2 - true or false?

Put a ring around true or false.

1. A minim is worth 4 beats. ................................................................... true     false

2. ♩ + ♩ + ♩ = 𝅗𝅥. ....................................................................................... true     false

3. There are 6 cello strings. ............................................................ true     false

4. The lowest cello string is C. ...................................................... true     false

5. This note is drawn correctly. 𝄢 ............................................... true     false

6. This is an A. 𝄢 ................................................................................ true     false

7. This is a semibreve. 𝅝 ................................................................. true     false

8. This is a line note. 𝄢 ................................................................... true     false

9. A treble bar goes at the end of a piece of music. ......................... true     false

10. This rest is worth 2 beats. ▬ ................................................. true     false

# Hey Presto!

**Hey Presto! Music theory for cellists:** books 1-6 are designed to take beginners on the cello up to at least Grade 1 theory level. With clear explanations, plenty of repetition and bags of fun, these workbooks give children a highly enjoyable introduction to music theory, relating it to their instrument, and building confidence right from the start.

**Other titles in the series:**

## Hey Presto! for violin

A comprehensive, step-by-step tutor series for young violinists. Attractive pieces and amusing characters and illustrations create enthusiasm and encourage musical expression, and clear, concise explanations give children and parents the information they need!

Why not visit www.heyprestostrings.com to see sample pages or listen to some of the pieces!

**Hey Presto! music for string groups:**

effective, imaginative compositions & arrangements suitable for performance - download instantly, and print as many parts as you need!

For more information, to see sample pages or listen to audio files, visit www.heyprestostrings.com

ISBN 978-0-9570449-4-4